How to Write

Writing Fiction

by Nick Rebman

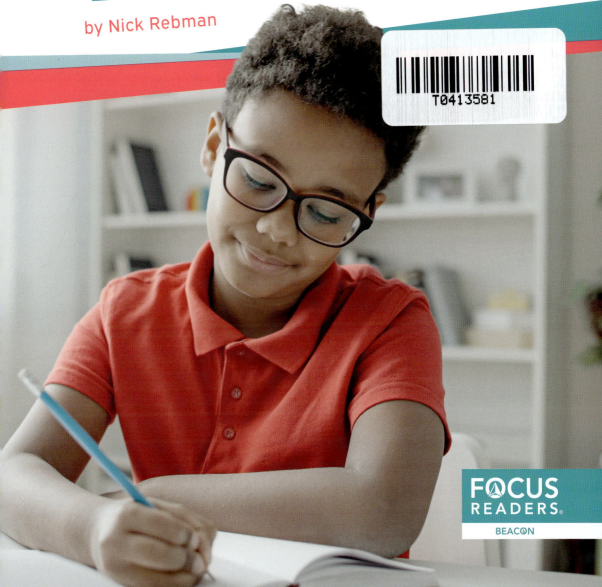

FOCUS READERS®
BEACON

www.focusreaders.com

Copyright © 2024 by Focus Readers®, Mendota Heights, MN 55120. All rights reserved. No part of this book may be reproduced or utilized in any form or by any means without written permission from the publisher.

Focus Readers is distributed by North Star Editions:
sales@northstareditions.com | 888-417-0195

Produced for Focus Readers by Red Line Editorial.

Photographs ©: Shutterstock Images, cover, 1, 4, 7, 8, 11, 12, 14, 17, 19, 20–21, 22, 25, 29; Red Line Editorial, 27

Library of Congress Cataloging-in-Publication Data
Names: Rebman, Nick, author.
Title: Writing fiction / by Nick Rebman.
Description: Mendota Heights, MN : Focus Readers, 2024. | Series: How to write | Includes bibliographical references and index. | Audience: Grades 2-3
Identifiers: LCCN 2023030829 (print) | LCCN 2023030830 (ebook) | ISBN 9798889980261 (hardcover) | ISBN 9798889980698 (paperback) | ISBN 9798889981527 (pdf) | ISBN 9798889981121 (ebook)
Subjects: LCSH: Fiction--Authorship--Juvenile literature. | Fiction--Technique--Juvenile literature.
Classification: LCC PN3355 .R33 2024 (print) | LCC PN3355 (ebook) | DDC 808.3--dc23/eng/20230809
LC record available at https://lccn.loc.gov/2023030829
LC ebook record available at https://lccn.loc.gov/2023030830

Printed in the United States of America
Mankato, MN
012024

About the Author

Nick Rebman is a writer and editor who lives in Minnesota.

Table of Contents

CHAPTER 1
Making a Plan 5

CHAPTER 2
Creating Conflict 9

CHAPTER 3
Rising Action 15

WRITE LIKE A PRO
Show, Don't Tell 20

CHAPTER 4
Revising and Editing 23

Focus on Writing Fiction • 28
Glossary • 30
To Learn More • 31
Index • 32

Chapter 1

Making a Plan

A boy has an idea for a story. So, he starts making notes. He lists the major events in his story. An astronaut crashes on a distant planet. Then an evil alien captures her. The astronaut has to escape.

Using sticky notes or index cards can help with writing. You can move events and ideas around easily.

Next, the boy makes notes about his characters. He describes what each one looks like. He describes their personalities. He also lists what they like and fear.

The boy makes notes about the **setting**, too. He lists many

One way to get ideas is to ask "what if" questions. For example, what if you arrived at school and nobody was there?

 Writing stories allows you to explore anything you can think of.

details about the alien's planet. He describes the sights and sounds.

The boy is happy with his plan. Now it's time to start writing!

Chapter 2

Creating Conflict

Writing **fiction** is a great way to use your imagination. Start by making a plan for your story. After that, it's time to work on the **first draft**. In this draft, try to write the whole story from start to finish.

 If you keep a notebook nearby, you can write down new ideas so you don't forget.

Don't focus on small details yet. Instead, just get through all the main events. You can always go back and change things later.

Start with a **scene** that will grab readers' attention. That way, people will want to keep reading. One way to do that is to make readers ask questions. For instance, you could describe a character in an odd situation. Readers will wonder how the situation started. Or you could begin with an exciting action scene.

 When readers wonder what will happen next, they'll keep reading. This is called suspense.

Readers will wonder if the character can escape.

The first scene should also introduce the story's main problem.

 A conflict in fiction can be like tug-of-war. Two sides have different goals. Only one succeeds.

This problem causes **conflict**.

Conflict makes stories fun to read.

Readers will want to see if the character can solve the problem.

The problem can take many forms. For example, characters might be searching for something. Or they might disagree with someone. Characters might also be trying to survive. Whatever you choose, the problem is what gets the story moving.

Did You Know?

A story usually has an event that starts the main conflict. This event is called the inciting incident.

Chapter 3

Rising Action

The **rising action** follows a story's conflict. The main character should be trying to reach her goal. But many things should get in the way. In fact, her problems should keep getting worse and worse.

 Unexpected events help make the story exciting. But make sure these events fit with the story.

Maybe she breaks her leg. Maybe she gets in a fight with her friend. She might plan for some problems. Others may be surprises.

This action might happen during several scenes. In each scene, try using **dialogue**. Dialogue can show a character's personality. Suppose

Read your dialogue out loud. That can help you figure out if the dialogue sounds real.

 Dialogue can show a character's background, emotions, and more.

a girl says, "I'd be happy to help you, sir." This could show she is kind and polite. Dialogue can also show how a character is feeling.

Suppose a man says, "I'll never be able to clean up this mess!" This could show he is frustrated.

Finally, your story needs an ending. Does the main character achieve his goal? Or does he fail? Maybe he finds the treasure he's looking for. But then he realizes he doesn't actually want it. What does he learn from this experience?

Often, the main character has to make a big decision at the end. This decision shows how

 Sometimes a character's big decision is between two very different choices.

she has changed. Perhaps a time traveler decides to stay in the past. Why does she make this choice? The writer's job is to help readers understand.

WRITE LIKE A PRO

Show, Don't Tell

Stories are more interesting when the reader can picture what's happening. Suppose you wrote, "Paul felt angry. His bike had been stolen." These sentences tell what happened. But they don't create a clear picture in the reader's mind. So, the reader may find it boring.

Now, suppose you wrote, "Paul's face turned bright red. He pounded his fist on the empty bike rack. 'It's gone!' he yelled." These sentences show what happened. The word *angry* isn't even used. But the reader can easily picture Paul's anger.

People show their emotions through their bodies.

Chapter 4

Revising and Editing

Your first draft is finished. Now it's time to **revise** and **edit**. Imagine someone is reading your story for the first time. Is there anything they might find confusing? If so, you'll need to explain it better.

 Some writers go through many drafts before they feel their stories are finished.

First, make sure all the events happen in a clear order. Use words like *before*, *after*, *during*, and *finally*. You can also use phrases like *the next day* or *an hour later*.

Next, think about your story's details. Details can help readers

Did You Know?

Many writers share drafts of their stories with friends they trust. Those friends tell what they liked. They also say what they found unhelpful or confusing.

 Helpful details might describe sights, smells, or sounds.

understand the characters. Details can also make a setting seem more real. However, not all details are necessary. Sometimes they can be distracting. So, get rid of details that don't help your story.

Then, make sure your story uses interesting verbs. Suppose you wrote, "Sarah went home." The verb *went* is boring. It doesn't describe the action very well. Was Sarah in a hurry? If so, you could write, "Sarah sprinted home." Or maybe she was hurt. You could write, "Sarah limped home."

Finally, read your story one last time. Fix any spelling mistakes. Then save a clean copy. Now your story is ready to print or share!

PARTS OF A STORY

action verb

Feelings that are shown, not told

scene

conflict

dialogue

ordering words

big decision

Skipping Space School

Frankie slammed on the super-speed button. Her spaceship zoomed away from school. Planets whizzed by. Why teleport to school for a silly astronaut test?

Just then, Frankie heard a loud thud. Then another. Oh no. She was flying through an asteroid belt!

Boom. A big space rock burst through one of the ship's engines. She had to crash land!

Frankie headed for the nearest planet. She hadn't learned how to crash land yet. Her eyes squeezed tight. The ship would crash any second . . .

Frankie frowned. No crash. She looked up. Mom?

"Frankie Blastoff the Third," her mom said. "We knew you snuck off this morning. So we turned the safety shields on around the planets. Just in case."

Frankie started to cry. "I'm so sorry," she said.

Her mom said, "You have a choice. You can go back home. Or you can go to school."

Frankie sighed. "Okay. School it is."

One second later, Frankie was in class. The lesson today? Crash Landing.

27

FOCUS ON
Writing Fiction

Write your answers on a separate piece of paper.

1. Write a paragraph that explains the main ideas of Chapter 4.

2. What type of conflict do you think is most interesting? Why?

3. When should you fix spelling mistakes?
    - **A.** when you're making notes
    - **B.** when you're writing the first draft
    - **C.** when you're editing

4. What is most likely to happen if you tell instead of show?
    - **A.** The reader will love the story.
    - **B.** The reader will get bored.
    - **C.** The reader will be confused.

5. What does **achieve** mean in this book?

*Finally, your story needs an ending. Does the main character **achieve** his goal? Or does he fail?*

    A. to have success
    B. to make mistakes
    C. to stop trying

6. What does **distracting** mean in this book?

*However, not all details are necessary. Sometimes they can be **distracting**.*

    A. impossible to understand
    B. not giving enough information
    C. taking attention away from what's important

Answer key on page 32.

Glossary

conflict
When someone wants something but can't get it.

dialogue
Talking, especially as part of a story.

edit
To improve a piece of writing by fixing mistakes.

fiction
Stories that describe made-up people or events.

first draft
The earliest form of a piece of writing. It will be changed and improved later.

revise
To improve a piece of writing by adding or removing details.

rising action
The part of a story where the problem gets worse or more intense.

scene
A specific place and time described in a story.

setting
The location and time in which a story takes place.

To Learn More

BOOKS

Eason, Sarah, and Louise Spilsbury. *How Do I Write Well?* Shrewsbury, UK: Cheriton Children's Books, 2022.

Heinrichs, Ann. *Similes and Metaphors*. Mankato, MN: The Child's World, 2020.

Minden, Cecilia, and Kate Roth. *Writing a Mystery*. Ann Arbor, MI: Cherry Lake Publishing, 2020.

NOTE TO EDUCATORS

Visit **www.focusreaders.com** to find lesson plans, activities, links, and other resources related to this title.

Index

C
characters, 6, 10–13, 15–18, 25
conflict, 12–13, 15, 27

D
details, 7, 10, 24–25
dialogue, 16–17, 27

E
editing, 23
ending, 18

F
feelings, 17, 27
first draft, 9, 23

I
inciting incident, 13

M
main character, 15, 18

N
notes, 5–6

O
ordering words, 24, 27

P
problems, 11–13, 15–16

R
rising action, 15

S
scenes, 10–11, 16, 27
sentences, 20
setting, 6–7, 25

V
verbs, 26–27

Answer Key: **1.** Answers will vary; **2.** Answers will vary; **3.** C; **4.** B; **5.** A; **6.** C

32